Kathleen and Oona
of Little Heather Island

By William S. Smith

Illustrated by Nancy J. Mayer
The artwork was created with watercolor and ink.

Published by Soixante Marque, LLC

Book Design and Editing by Colleen A. Patterson

For Meegan and Sydney

CONTENTS

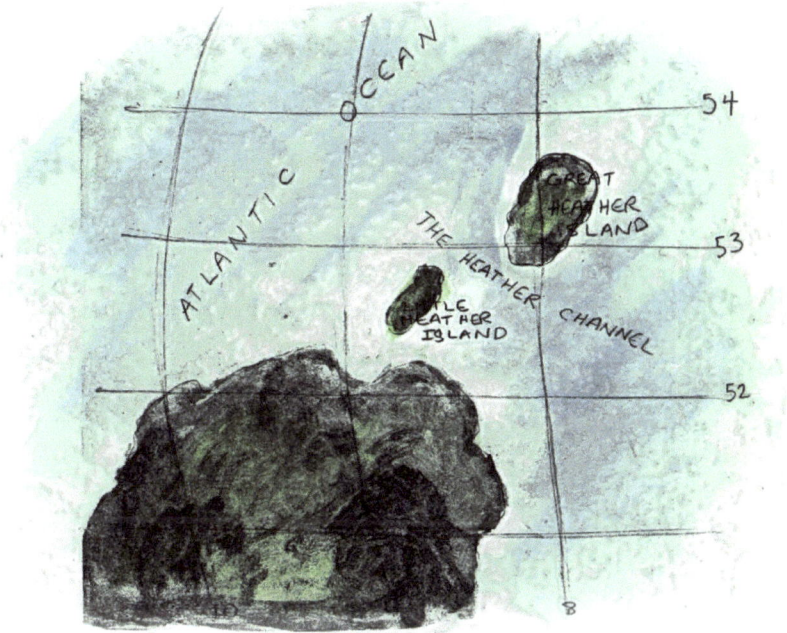

1. Change on the Horizon

When Kathleen Higgins was seven-years-old, her father told her that the King had given him a new assignment. King Henry had asked Captain Higgins to assume the post of Lord Protector of Little Heather Island, which was two miles to the west of The Great Heather Island, where they lived in the North Atlantic Ocean. They would need to move there, her father said, but they would have

1

the good fortune of living in a large stone house overlooking the sea. Her father also told her that the King had arranged for them to have a full-time housekeeper who would prepare their meals and attend to all of their needs while he was busy with his duties as Lord Protector. When Kathleen's mother died the year before, the King had given Captain Higgins permission to stay at home with his daughter for a year to comfort her and help her adjust to life without her mother's gracious and loving presence. Now he was needed to help run the country.

"And Kathleen," Captain Higgins said as he affectionately pulled one of her copper-colored pigtails, "once we settle into our new home, I have a special surprise planned for the two of us." While Kathleen was sorry to be leaving the only home she had ever known, she smiled sweetly at her father because she knew life was full of many sudden changes for him too.

2. A New Home

After the ferryboat delivered Captain Higgins with Kathleen and their station wagon to Little Heather Island on the day of their big move, they drove along the quaint little harbor for only a short distance before coming to the grand entrance gate of their new and mysterious-looking home. The entire estate was surrounded by an eight-foot-high stone wall. When her father announced their arrival with a honk of the car horn, a man in uniform stepped out of the stone gatehouse, saluted him, and opened the large wrought-iron gate. Kathleen and Captain Higgins then drove up the crushed stone path leading to the main house and their new life.

When Kathleen first set her eyes on their new home, she was overwhelmed. She thought it was more like a castle. It had ten bedrooms, six bathrooms, four large reception halls, and the most enormous kitchen she had ever seen. The dining room table was so massive that it was surrounded by twenty high-backed chairs. How silly she and her father would look when they had dinner by themselves in that formal room every night! Instead of making her feel like a princess, she was a bit afraid that living there might only make her feel more lonely and small.

Kathleen managed to adjust to the new conditions on Little Heather Island without any fuss because she loved her father and knew he dearly missed her mother too and she longed for them to have a peaceful and happy life. Mrs. Murphy, the housekeeper, was a warm and kind lady who was forever baking cookies or preparing little snacks for them to take on their walks around the property inside the big walls. Sometimes they would venture out as far as the little village and stop for hot chocolate in the sweets shop. Kathleen was shy and reluctant to ask the guard at the gatehouse to open the front gate, but Mrs. Murphy told her it was no bother because it was his job to do so.

By order of the King, the children of The Heather Islands did not have to begin school until they were seven-and-a-half years old. That was still two months away for Kathleen and she was

disappointed that with Christmas coming soon, she wouldn't have any classmates yet to share the holidays with. She knew that Mrs. Murphy was doing everything she could to make her feel happy and cared for, but it just wasn't the same without her mother's special kind of love. And she didn't want to bother her father with her doubts because she knew he was very occupied with his new responsibilities. It seemed he had even forgotten the special surprise he had promised her.

3. Christmas

But then everything changed on Christmas morning. Kathleen awakened when she heard a strange scraping sound at her bedroom door. When she looked at the alarm clock and saw that it was seven o'clock, the time to rise and look under the Christmas tree, she sprang out of bed and flung open her door. She couldn't believe her eyes! Two large gray puppies came hurtling into her room playfully knocking her over and licking her face.

"Merry Christmas, Kathleen!" her father bellowed exuberantly as he followed the puppies into her room sporting his best smile. "Did you think I could ever forget the special surprise I promised you?"

"Daddy, Daddy, are these puppies for me? I love them, they're so cute and friendly. What kind of doggies are they? They look just like you. Look, they have the same gray beard you have." Kathleen was so excited that all of her words came tumbling out at once, causing her father to laugh.

"Well, Kathleen," he said, "remember when I said the surprise would be for both of us? The puppy you are petting is the male, and he will be my dog. The female, the one who's licking your face, is your doggie. They're Irish Wolfhounds, known to be the noblest breed of dogs on earth.

The most wonderful trait of Wolfhounds is their complete dedication to their mistress or master, so I expect you two will become very close friends."

Captain Higgins and Kathleen spent all Christmas day romping with their new puppies. Kathleen was so thrilled and overjoyed that she didn't remember to look under the Christmas tree until lunchtime. There she found three boxes, each with her name on it. One contained a lovely pink dressing robe, the second a dainty handmade porcelain doll from England, but the third one was her favorite. Inside was a handsome leather leash and dog collar bearing a silver medallion with the name "Oona" engraved on it. "Oona?" she asked her father. "Is that to be my dog's name?"

"Sit with me, Dear, and let me tell you a story," said her father.

4. The Legend Behind Oona's Name

Captain Higgins told Kathleen about the legendary Irish hero, Finn McCool, a mighty warrior who defended his country and people with honor from all sorts of foreign invaders. "He was a very noble and courageous man," the Captain explained, "and he possessed many of the traits that the Irish Wolfhound is also famous for. According to folklore, Kathleen, Finn's wife was named Oona, and she helped him outwit and overcome the evil giant Cuchulain many years ago. "I thought," he said, "that we should name our two dogs after Finn and Oona, and they can protect us just like the legendary Finn and Oona, on our own island kingdom."

Kathleen was delighted with her father's idea
and so the new names fit perfectly. Later that day,
Captain Higgins explained to her what her new
responsibilities toward the dogs would be. She was
to always be sure that they each had a full bowl of
fresh water. Both puppies needed to be walked on
their leashes every morning, afternoon and night
until their legs became strong enough to run on
their own around the property. Her father said he
would accompany her when his duties to the King

allowed and that Mrs. Murphy had agreed to take his place when he was too busy to walk with her and the dogs. Her biggest and most complex job was to make sure that they were fed the proper food three times a day until they were one-year-old.

He handed Kathleen a list of the ingredients for each meal:

- 2 cups dry kibble
- 1 tablespoon vitamin C powder
- 1 tablespoon mixed herbs from their garden (peppermint, basil, dandelion and nettles)
- 2 tablespoons slippery elm powder
- 1 tablespoon kelp
- 1 tablespoon wheat germ
- 1 tablespoon plain yogurt
- 1 tablespoon raw honey

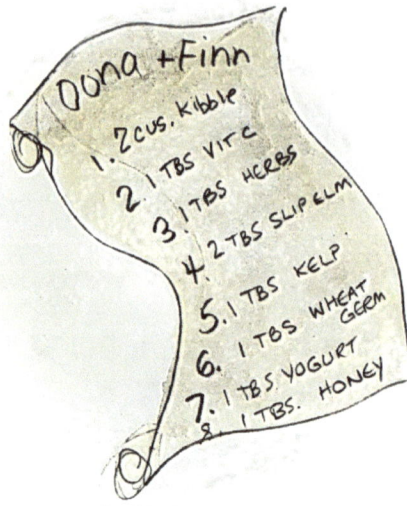

Oona + Finn
1. 2 cus. Kibble
2. 1 TBS Vit C
3. 1 TBS Herbs
4. 2 TBS Slip Elm
5. 1 TBS Kelp
6. 1 TBS Wheat Germ
7. 1 TBS Yogurt
8. 1 TBS. Honey

And for their evening meal, her father said, she should add nine ounces of raw beef hearts. "Mix it all together, Kathleen, and stir in two tablespoons of olive oil and some water to make it moist and to give them shiny coats," he added.

Kathleen took to her new responsibilities with relish. Both Finn and Oona grew stronger and more beautiful every day and by the summer, they were sufficiently developed that she and her father began to take them on longer and longer walks. Their favorite path soon took them beyond the walls of their estate down the road leading to the seawall. Kathleen and her father would always stop there for a moment and look out over the sea to The Great Heather Island and watch the shimmering light on the water. Many times her father would take her hand. They rarely talked about it, but Kathleen always thought of her own sweet mother at these times. They both missed her dearly.

Kathleen noticed one day that if she and her father lingered too long at this spot on the seawall, Finn and Oona would gently nudge them with their heads. To her, it was like they were saying, "Don't be sad. Come along with us. We'll protect you and make you happy."

After the dogs passed their first birthday, her father was so pleased with the skillful way she had trained them that he suggested they celebrate by letting Oona and Finn walk freely alongside them without leashes. From then on, when they reached

their spot at the seawall, after a few moments, the dogs would nudge their master and mistress and then run off together to the end of the promenade and return to them for some spirited cavorting and petting. It became a regular routine that both Kathleen and her father cherished.

5. Life on Little Heather Island

Over the next two years, there were many amazing developments in Kathleen's young life. She had begun school in the village and every day would ride her bicycle down the hill from her house to the front gate, call to Mr. Murphy to open it for her (she had soon found out that he was Mrs. Murphy's husband!), grin and wave respectfully to him and then pedal off to the schoolhouse. She made many splendid friends at class, and had begun to go horseback riding with them on weekends. Her father had arranged for her to take piano lessons, and every Tuesday afternoon, her inspiring and encouraging piano teacher would come to the house and give her a lesson. Joy was bubbling through Kathleen's little world.

Another big change for Kathleen was that her father had become extremely busy as Lord Protector of Little Heather Island and was often away for days at a time when the King summoned him to his castle on The Great Heather Island. At these times Kathleen would go on her daily jaunts with Finn and Oona accompanied by Mrs. Murphy.

Kathleen noticed that when her father was away, Finn would stop on his own at the spot on the seawall, and look toward The Great Heather Island, as if he was sensing his master was there. On these occasions, Oona would nudge both

Kathleen and Finn in order to break the spell. Then
they would run off together, as always, feeling the
magic in their hearts and twinkles in their eyes.
Over the next few years, Kathleen grew deeply
attached to her beloved Finn and Oona. Every
night, the two precious dogs would take their
positions on opposite sides outside her bedroom
door, like two giant lions guarding the entrance.
When Kathleen did her homework in the
afternoons after school, Oona and Finn would sleep
on the floor beside her. Every once in a while,

Oona would get up and rest her immense head on the desk, next to the spot where Kathleen was working. If Kathleen didn't break her concentration and reach over to scratch Oona after a minute or so, the dog would nudge her arm until she got the attention she longed for.

At Christmastime one year Kathleen invented a new game to play with Oona. One day when she was shopping in the village with Mrs. Murphy, she was ecstatic to find a pair of cloth antlers that could be fastened onto the dog's head by means of an elastic strap. "Perfect!" she giggled to Mrs. Murphy. "I want to buy these for Oona. She'll look just like a reindeer."

When she got home, she secured the cloth antlers on Oona, which sent Finn into a fit of barking. It was hilarious! When Captain Higgins returned home that evening, he took a picture of

both dogs with Oona wearing the antlers. They loved it so much that they had lots of copies made to use as Christmas cards.

6. To the Veterinarian

A couple of weeks later, Captain Higgins was away overnight on The Great Heather Island when Kathleen and Mrs. Murphy took Finn and Oona out at sunset for their evening walk. After the dogs galloped off from their special spot on the seawall, Kathleen noticed that Oona was limping when she returned. She looked at her front right leg and noticed a large bump near the ankle. Mrs. Murphy said that when Captain Higgins got home, he would arrange to take Oona to the veterinarian to have her examined.

Later that night, after Kathleen had gotten into bed, she thought about Oona again and was worried. She got out of bed and opened her door and saw that Finn was licking the bump on Oona's leg. Her heart smiled. Her dogs were her dearest of friends.

When her father returned home to Little
Heather Island the next day, Kathleen told him
about Oona's leg. Captain Higgins looked
concerned; she could see it in his eyes. He told her
he would take Oona right away to Dr. Alexander,
the veterinarian. He said she could come with them
if she wished and cautioned her that Oona's
problem might be serious.

After examining Oona's leg and doing the appropriate medical tests, the veterinarian sat down with Kathleen and her father. "I'm very sorry to tell you this, but I think Oona might have a cancerous condition in her leg. After I have this tissue sample studied at the laboratory, I will know for sure."

Captain Higgins and Kathleen were silent when they took Oona home that afternoon. As she sat beside her father, Kathleen took deep breaths as she smiled gently at Oona in the backseat.

When they returned home, her father told her that he hoped that they would hear from Dr. Alexander in the morning. "Until then," he said, "try to be as natural as possible with Oona in every way. We don't want her to know that we're upset. She wouldn't like that as she is your Protectress."

7. Being Strong for Oona

Kathleen didn't sleep well that night. She couldn't stop thinking about Oona. Her father stayed home from work the next morning to wait for Dr. Alexander's call. After the veterinarian called, Captain Higgins took Kathleen into his study.

Kathleen's father sat in his big reading chair and asked Kathleen to sit next to him on the ottoman. "Kathleen Dear," he said, "the news is not good. The cancer is not just in Oona's leg; it has spread to much of her body. Dr. Alexander said our Oona doesn't have very long to live."

All the fear that Kathleen had kept inside herself suddenly came to the surface and burst forth and she threw her arms around her father's neck. She sobbed and sobbed for a long time, while he held her and kept patting her on the head. Finally, she asked "Is Oona in a lot of pain?'

"No," her father said. "But according to Dr. Alexander, she may be soon."

"That's not fair," Kathleen cried. "She's been such a good dog for four years. She was always so attentive to us if we were sad, trying to cheer us up when we missed Mother. How can I help her and be as good to her now that she is sick?"

"I asked Dr. Alexander that same question, Kathleen. He's a very good veterinarian and knows how much we love Oona. He said that nothing can be done now to save her, as her leg is in danger of breaking. Because of their great size, an Irish Wolfhound can't live without all four legs."

"What he said we must do, Kathleen, to be fair to her, is to bring Oona in to him when she shows the first sign of distress. An Irish Wolfhound will hide pain from her mistress until it becomes too difficult, because they feel their main purpose is to be protective. When she gives you that sign, we should take her to Dr. Alexander so he can help her by giving her a shot that will send her to doggie heaven."

Kathleen cried all over again. "I can't believe how good she is. She knows her pain makes me feel sad, and so she suffers silently. She's so brave!"

The next morning when Kathleen was petting Oona after she fed her, Oona looked away for a moment and sighed the deepest sigh that Kathleen had ever heard. She even thought she saw a tear forming in Oona's right eye. She ran quickly to her father and told him. Later that morning, they took Oona to Dr. Alexander where she died peacefully in their loving arms. It was a sorrowful day. Now it was Kathleen's turn to be brave.

The law of The Heather Islands required that all animals be cremated after death. Captain Higgins worked with Dr. Alexander to make these arrangements.

Two days later, Captain Higgins took Kathleen with him to walk Finn for the first time since Oona had died. When they got to their spot on the seawall, he told Kathleen that the King had given him permission to spread Oona's ashes in the sea between The Great Heather Island and Little Heather Island. She stood there, eyes wet with tears, and stared for a longer time than usual. Finn fixed his gaze out over the waters with her, the way he used to when Captain Higgins was away on the other island. This time it was Captain Higgins who finally nudged Finn and sent him on his way to the end of the pier. Finn never ran faster.

Captain Higgins told Kathleen that from that day forward, he wanted her to walk Finn by herself for him. "After all," he said, "you will be twelve-years-old in a few months. And you need Finn's companionship now as much as he needs yours."

In fact, after they stopped at the seawall together every day, Kathleen started running with Finn to the end of the pier and back just like Oona had. That made them both feel better.

8. A Happy Surprise

On the morning of her twelfth birthday, Kathleen took Finn on their usual morning walk. When they returned to the front gate leading to their house, Mr. and Mrs. Murphy were both waiting to let them in. "Your father wants to see you right away in the garden behind the house," Mrs. Murphy said with a liltingly expectant tone.

Captain Higgins called out to her as soon as she turned the corner of the house. "Kathleen, hurry. Someone is here to see you!"

And who was that someone but a little, gray, female Irish Wolfhound puppy who looked just like Oona! Life was new again!

It was one of the happiest days in Kathleen Higgins' life. And it was definitely one of the happiest days in Captain Higgins' life.

Kathleen named her new puppy "Happy" which was the perfect name and how she wanted to feel forever.

For the next several months, she repeated with Happy all the things she had learned about caring for an Irish Wolfhound puppy when Finn and Oona had first arrived. She knew that she would have to wait a few months before Happy could come along with her and Finn on the long walk to the seawall.

Two months later, Captain Higgins came home from work early one afternoon and asked Kathleen if she thought that Happy was ready for a long walk yet. "Oh, I'd love to take Happy, Father," she sang. And off they went.

When they all got to their special spot on the seawall, Kathleen and her father both looked across the sea as always. Captain Higgins reached for his daughter's hand and they shared quiet memories. After a few minutes, Finn barked and nudged Captain Higgins first and then Kathleen with his large head. Then he sat down, very excitedly.

"What is it, Finn?" Captain Higgins wondered out loud.

"I know what he wants, Father," Kathleen said. She removed Happy's leash and looked over at Finn.

Finn barked again and went over and nuzzled Happy. The next minute both dogs were running together down to the end of the pier. Captain Higgins and Kathleen laughed with abandon, smiled tenderly at each other, and ran off after them.

About the Author:

William S. Smith was born into a seafaring family. A New York native, he currently resides in Charleston, South Carolina.

About the Illustrator:

Nancy J. Mayer is a freelance illustrator whom Mr. Smith met over 30 years ago. They have collaborated on a number of projects.

www.ingramcontent.com/pod-product-compliance
Lightning Source LLC
Chambersburg PA
CBHW041802040426
42448CB00001B/13